>>> SKITS FOR STUDENT MINISTRY

ILLUSTRATE
BIBLE TRUTHS
FROM ANOTHER ANGLE

12 SKETCHES
12 SKETCHES

Standard®
PUBLISHING
Bringing the Word to Life™
Cincinnati, Ohio

Published by Standard Publishing, Cincinnati, Ohio

www.standardpub.com

Copyright © 2008 Standard Publishing

Printed in: USA

Project editor: Kelly Carr

Cover and interior design: The DesignWorks Group

ISBN 978-0-7847-2252-7

14 13 12 11 10 09 08   9 8 7 6 5 4 3 2 1

CONTENTS

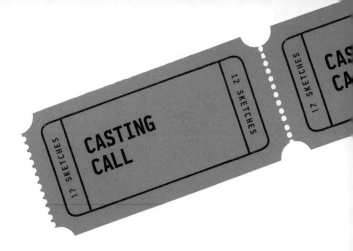

We're glad you picked up this book. These sketches take important Bible truths and illustrate them with unique, current perspectives. There are parodies of popular culture as well as realistic teen situations to draw students into the action.

Stories resonate with students. By constructing modern-day stories from truths found in the Bible, the ideas will capture teens' attention and stick in their minds. Those acting out the skits as well as those watching will realize that the topics found in God's Word truly ARE relevant to their daily lives!

We all know students who have a dramatic flair for life. That's who we had in mind when we created these skits. Each skit is designed for teens to use their skills in dramatizing concepts found in the Bible that remain relevant to their lives today. These skits are limited—in a good way: limited to a few cast members, a few lines to learn, and a few props.

So whether you are capping off a youth group talk, reiterating a retreat session, applying a Sunday school lesson, or reinforcing a sermon, the skits in this book will get your teens in on the act!

>>> **PURPOSE:**

Use this parody of *American Idol* to illustrate a discussion about rejection.

>>> **POSSIBLE SCRIPTURES:**

Deuteronomy 31:1-6
1 Samuel 8:1-22

>>> **PROPS:**

table
three chairs

>>> **PEOPLE:** *(IMITATING THE* AMERICAN IDOL *CAST)*

RILEY PIECRUST—enthusiastic host (imitating Ryan Seacrest)
RODNEY—laid-back contest judge (imitating Randy Jackson)
PATTY—overly happy contest judge (imitating Paula Abdul)
SILAS—snobby British contest judge (imitating Simon Cowell)
SAMANTHA—teen singing contestant

RODNEY, PATTY, and SILAS are sitting behind a table. The table should be toward one side of the stage, angled so all three can be seen by audience but so that when SAMANTHA *enters and performs for them, she can face the table but not have her back completely to the audience. RILEY stands center stage, facing the audience.*

RILEY: *[to audience, talks with jovial tone as if everything he says is funny]* Hello, everyone, and welcome back to *Hometown Idol*, the show where we travel to your hometown and search for the best singing talent that could possibly exist in such a remote area. Believe me, that's easier said than done! *[smiles with a big cheesy grin]* I'm your host, Riley Piecrust! Today we're somewhere in the Midwest—it's hard to keep track exactly where. All these towns look the same! But anyway, things are heating up tonight as we continue the auditions. Let's see who will make the cut. But before we do, let's check in with our judges. The talented Rodney . . . *[walks over to the judges' table and gestures to RODNEY]*

RODNEY: *[does peace sign hand gesture]* What's up, dog?!

RILEY: The lovely Patty. *[gestures to PATTY]*

PATTY: Hi! I love everyone! *[stands and blows kisses to audience]*

RILEY: That's great, Patty. And the opinionated Silas. *[gestures to SILAS]*

SILAS: *[hands folded across chest]* I don't like anyone.

RILEY: Yes, we've figured that out, Silas. You're about as sweet as a lemon. *[walks back to center stage and speaks to audience]* And don't forget, I'm your host, Riley Piecrust! *[pauses for dramatic effect and gives another big cheesy grin]* We're ready to kick off with a new batch of contestants for the evening. And I can tell our judges are excited!

[RILEY looks over at the judges, and all three look discouraged, shaking their heads no, putting their hands over their faces, or similar actions.]

RILEY: Who will impress? Who will distress? Our first audition for the night is Samantha. Let's watch as Samantha makes her way in to perform for the judges.

[RILEY exits off the side where the judges are, as SAMANTHA enters from the opposite side. SAMANTHA stands to face the judges but should not have her back to the audience.]

RODNEY: Hey, hey, hey. First audition of the night. What's your name?

SAMANTHA: Samantha.

PATTY: Hey, Samantha! Start us off right, girl!

SILAS: Please just don't be horrible.

RODNEY: Samantha, why do you want to be the next Hometown Idol?

SAMANTHA: Because I love to sing, and I'm a hard worker.

PATTY: You go, girl! Never give up on your dreams, honey.

SILAS: All right. Enough with this love fest. Can we get down to business and let the girl sing? That's what she came to do.

PATTY: You're always so negative, Silas.

SILAS: And you're a little too *perky*, Patty.

RODNEY: All right, all right, you two. Samantha, why don't you break it down for us?

SAMANTHA: OK. Here it goes. *[singing enthusiastically but slightly off key]* "Amazing grace, how sweet the sound, that saved a wretch like me."

SILAS: *[interrupting]* Wretch? Her singing is *wretch*-ed!

PATTY: Silas, be quiet! Let her finish. *[smiles at SAMANTHA]* Go on, sweetie.

SAMANTHA: *[singing a little better this time]* "I once was lost, but now I'm found, was blind but now I see."

SILAS: I wish I was deaf and couldn't hear!

PATTY: Silas! She has amazing passion.

SILAS: I want to know what she did with the money.

PATTY: What money?

SILAS: The money her mother gave her for singing lessons.

RODNEY: Dude, she's not that bad.

SILAS: Not bad? She sounds like she's doing bad karaoke on a cruise ship! I say she shouldn't go on to Hollywood. She's decent at best but not star quality. The recording industry would eat her alive.

PATTY: And I say she should go. You're pouring your heart out, Samantha, and people will love that about you. You're being who you are, and that's the most important thing.

RODNEY: Looks like I'm the deciding vote. Samantha, I'm gonna be honest, it was a little pitchy for me. You've got some potential, but you're just not there yet. I'm gonna have to say no.

[RILEY enters again as RODNEY finishes his last line.]

RODNEY: Go and work on your voice some more.

[SAMANTHA turns and walks away from the table as RILEY steps over to her and guides her toward her exit side of the stage, closer to the audience, away from the judges' earshot. The three judges pantomime talking to each other as the skit ends.]

RILEY: Samantha, you've just been rejected. You're not going to Hollywood. How do you feel?

SAMANTHA: Wow. I know I'm not the best singer in the world, but Silas was a little harsh!

RILEY: Yeah, he's like that a lot. We just ignore him. So, what will you do now?

SAMANTHA: *[disappointed but not shaken]* This is hard. I mean, singing is my dream. But I'm not giving up. I've been singing in church my whole life. I may not be good enough right now to sing in Hollywood, but I know God will always enjoy hearing me sing his praises! After all, he tells us to make a joyful noise. I guess that noise doesn't always have to be on key!

RILEY: If you say so, Samantha. *[to audience, says next lines dramatically]* You heard it here, folks. Samantha was *pressed* but not crushed. *Struck down* but not destroyed. *Rejected* but not in despair. The emotion! The drama! We're heading for a commercial break, but we'll have lots more audition footage—the beauties and the beasts—when we return here on *Hometown Idol*. Remember, I'm your host, Riley Piecrust, and soon I'll be coming to a hometown near you. *[points to audience as he says "you" and gives a big cheesy grin]*

>>> **PURPOSE:**

Use this parody of MTV's *Made* to illustrate a discussion about how people can take a stand for God.

>>> **POSSIBLE SCRIPTURES:**

1 Kings 18:18-38
Mark 14:66-72
Acts 4:1-22

>>> **PROPS:**

podium or music stand that can be easily carried on and off stage
uniforms or matching shorts and shirts for CUB SCOUTS
long sticks that could be used to roast food over a campfire
small dining table
chairs—for all LUNCH FRIENDS plus one
(optional) stool for narrator

>>> **PEOPLE:**

NARRATOR—male or female
ANDRÉ—average teen
COACH JOSHUA—average guy, older than André

DEBATER—female; nonspeaking role

CUB SCOUTS—two or three males acting like kids; nonspeaking roles

LUNCH FRIENDS—three or four people, males and females; nonspeaking roles

NARRATOR is off to one side during the entire skit and may sit on a stool or stand. NARRATOR says all lines to the audience. ANDRÉ enters and stands center stage as NARRATOR begins. ANDRÉ remains centrally located while all other characters come and go.

NARRATOR: André is a sophomore in high school who admits that he's not as bold as he wants to be. When people say and do things that go against God's truths, André knows that he should take a stand, but he hasn't had the courage to try. So André wants to be *[emphasize word since it's the name of the show]* CREATED into a teen with a backbone! His goal is to be able to take a stand for God. Our show *Created* provided André with a coach who shaped him up to get ready to take a stand! Did André find the courage in just six weeks? Watch and find out!

ANDRÉ: *[to audience]* I know I should be more bold and live out my faith better. But it's hard to do. I'm not that courageous. So I signed up for *Created*. I want to be created into a person ready to take a stand for God. The hardest thing for me is when someone starts talking bad about God or making fun of Christians. I want to say something, but I chicken out. I think people around me know that I go to church and all, but do they really see that my faith is a part of my everyday life? I'm not so sure.

NARRATOR: André's first task is meeting his *Created* coach. His name is Joshua.

ANDRÉ: *[to audience]* I'm picturing some huge guy who will yell at me like a drill sergeant.

[COACH JOSHUA enters and walks up to shake ANDRÉ's hand as he speaks.]

COACH JOSHUA: Hey, André. I'm your coach, Joshua. Are you ready to be *Created*?

ANDRÉ: Wow! You're my coach? You're different than I expected!

COACH JOSHUA: What do you mean?

ANDRÉ: I thought you'd be some big, scary guy. But you're just an average guy like me.

Coach Joshua: That's right, André. You don't have to be a huge, tough-talking, angry-sounding bully to take a stand for God. In fact, that approach can turn people away from God. I'm here to show you that any average guy can have the confidence to take a stand. And you can do it in a way that's honorable so that other people will notice something different about you.

André: Cool.

Coach Joshua: Now I've got a series of tasks that you're going to complete in the next six weeks. It will take hard work, but you can do it.

André: *[to audience]* Coach Joshua was right. The tasks were intimidating, and it took a lot of hard work. The first thing I had to do was join the debate team. Coach Joshua said I needed to practice my skills of putting what I believe into words. I was really nervous.

[As André says his next lines, Debater enters with podium in hand and sets it near André and Coach Joshua. She begins pantomiming that she is debating.]

André: *[to audience]* My first assigned debate was to argue why the school should give students an extra minute between classes to get to our lockers and on to our next class. That sounded simple enough, but I was going up against a veteran on the debate team. *[to Joshua]* Coach Joshua, I don't know if I can do this or not. I don't like getting up in front of people.

[As Coach Joshua speaks, Debater steps aside and he guides André to step behind the podium.]

Coach Joshua: You'll only be doing this practice debate in front of the debate team. You'll be fine. You've prepared well. You've practiced with me a bunch. And you believe in your topic. That's the most important thing—believing in what you've got to say. That's the kind of passion and confidence you'll need when you take a stand for God. This debate will get you ready.

[André says his next two sets of lines while standing behind the podium.]

André: Well, I wasn't perfect. The veteran girl on the debate team won the match.

[DEBATER smiles and waves to the audience, as if they congratulated her on her win.]

ANDRÉ: But I did get my points across and felt good for even making it through. The debate team sponsor said it was great for my first time. It did inspire me that I could get better and more confident about the things I said. I was up for whatever Coach Joshua threw my way next . . . or so I thought!

[As NARRATOR says next line, DEBATER exits, taking podium with her.]

NARRATOR: But André didn't have much time to enjoy his accomplishment. Coach Joshua was ready with his next assignment.

COACH JOSHUA: OK, André. Your second challenge is to go on an overnight camping experience with a group of Cub Scouts.

ANDRÉ: Are you kidding me? What am I supposed to learn from a bunch of little kids?

[As COACH JOSHUA says his next line, CUB SCOUTS enter carrying sticks and sit nearby in a semicircle, holding the sticks toward the middle of the circle, as if roasting food over a campfire. They pantomime roasting, talking, and laughing.]

COACH JOSHUA: The young scouts are mastering the art of being prepared. It's one of their mottos. And you need to be prepared because you never know when you'll have a chance to take a stand for God.

[ANDRÉ sits down next to the CUB SCOUTS, joining their semicircle. He stays there as he says his next lines.]

ANDRÉ: *[to audience]* Although I was still skeptical, the camping time with the Cub Scouts wasn't half bad. Those little guys did teach me a thing or two about being prepared.

[As NARRATOR says next line, CUB SCOUTS exit, taking their sticks with them. LUNCH FRIENDS enter, carrying the small table and one chair for each of them, plus one for ANDRÉ. They set up the table and chairs center stage and slouch into them (leaving a chair for ANDRÉ that faces the audience), as if relaxing at lunch. They pantomime eating, talking, and laughing.]

NARRATOR: After several more tasks and six weeks of hard work, Coach Joshua told André he was ready. Now the only thing André needed to do was go to school and be on the lookout for places to take a stand for God. A situation could come up at any moment.

[COACH JOSHUA shakes ANDRÉ's hand or pats his back, waves good-bye, and exits. As ANDRÉ says his next line, he sits down at the lunch table and stays there as he says his final lines.]

ANDRÉ: *[to audience]* It didn't take long for me to run into a conversation where all my new skills came into play. At lunch, I was sitting with my usual group of friends, when the topic of God came up. Immediately I thought of all the lessons Coach Joshua taught me. I thought about the debate team and how confident I felt when I spoke for something I believed in. I thought about the Cub Scouts and how I was prepared for this very moment.

[One FRIEND pantomimes talking as others stop to listen.]

ANDRÉ: *[to audience]* So one friend says something about how God is just an angry person up in the sky, waiting to strike people down for doing evil things. I knew this was my chance. *[to FRIEND]* "Actually, you've got the idea of God all wrong," I said. *[to audience]* And I went on to tell them all some stuff about how God wants a relationship with us and it breaks his heart when we do bad, because he loves us so much and wants the best for us.

[Another FRIEND, a male, pantomimes saying something to ANDRÉ.]

ANDRÉ: *[to audience]* No, they didn't all decide right then and there to become Christians or anything. But one guy seemed surprised at what I knew and asked me if he and I could talk some more later. He said he had some questions about God that he'd been thinking about recently. So already God has opened some doors for me—all because I got enough courage to take a stand for him. Looks like I'm a new man! I can't wait to tell Coach Joshua!

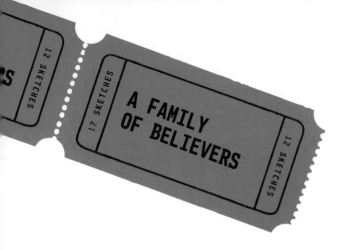

A FAMILY OF BELIEVERS

12 SKETCHES

Use this skit to illustrate a discussion about how modern churches do a good or a poor job of being the family of God.

>>> POSSIBLE SCRIPTURES:

Psalm 78:1-8
Matthew 12:46-50
John 1:12, 13
Acts 2:42-47
Ephesians 2:19

>>> PROPS:

table
four chairs
newspaper
(optional) For DAD to get the exact wording of each church description correct, and since DAD is supposed to be reading from the newspaper, you can photocopy and paste the pieces of his dialogue that describe the churches right into the prop newspaper for DAD to read directly from the page.

DAD
MOM
CHILD—male or female
TEEN—male or female

Family is sitting around a dinner table. Make sure no character's back is to the audience. Newspaper is on the table.

DAD: OK, kids. Now I know this move has been rough on you. New town, new school, new everything. But your mother and I think it will be easier once we find a church family to be a part of.

MOM: So we think that on our first Sunday here, we should decide together where we'll worship. Sound good?

CHILD: *[enthusiastically]* Sure!

TEEN: *[sounds forced into it]* OK. If we have to.

DAD: All right. Let's just look in the newspaper here *[opens paper in front of him]* and see what we can find. Here we are—ads for churches. I'll read a few, and we can decide what we like. First we have: *[reading]* "Country Club Church, the town's most exclusive religious establishment. Proud to offer a luxurious worship center for its members only. Dues provide members with opportunities for 18 holes of golf after the sermon. Members won't have to worry about being bothered by strays—we have a rigorous application process, and only the top candidates qualify."

TEEN: Sounds like a bunch of snobs!

CHILD: Do they have a pool?

DAD: Let's keep reading. How about this one? *[reading]* "First Church of the Museum Center and Gift Shop. We are *the* first church in the state. Come and see the actual pews where visiting former presidents were seated. Visit the exhibit where a Bible from the Gutenberg press is on display. Browse through our gift shop where you can purchase stained glass candleholders or replicas of our organ. Worship services also available once a month. Request a schedule in the gift shop."

MOM: Ohhh! That sounds interesting! I love antiques!

CHILD: *[in singsong voice]* Bo-ring!!!

TEEN: I'd rather just sleep in.

DAD: Here's another. *[reading]* "Come to Church USA! Must be an American citizen, a registered voter, and know all four stanzas of 'The Star-Spangled Banner.' You'll find us on Washington Avenue under the giant American flag."

MOM: *[unimpressed]* Keep going, honey.

DAD: OK. *[reading]* "Spotlight Community Church. Sing the top praise hits with the hottest worship band in the city! You'll be amazed by our state-of-the-art technology with surround sound, laser light show, and high-def videos for every song. You won't find sermons here—instead we offer movies and performances by our professional drama troupe, with short 'spiritual talks' afterward. All band members and actors are available after each show for photos and autographs. Nothing is required to attend except a $10 entry fee."

TEEN: Wow! That sounds cool!

MOM: *[displeased]* It sounds like a concert.

TEEN: Exactly. Can we go there? Please?!

DAD: Let's look at all our options. *[reading]* "The Smith family would like to welcome you to the Walter Smith Memorial Church. As the name indicates, Walter Smith founded this congregation decades ago, and his family has carried on the tradition since that time. Here you'll meet preacher Bob Smith, youth minister Randy Smith, children's director Deborah Smith Watson, and song leader Larry Smith." Hmmm. I'm not too sure about that one.

MOM: I don't know how much we'd be able to get involved there.

DAD: Here's an interesting ad. *[reading]* "Enlist at Fort Christian: Boot Camp for Believers. Step right up and get your marching orders as we drill you with the rules for living found in the Bible. Forget what you've heard at those mushy, warm, and fuzzy churches. Jesus is for people who work hard and *earn* the right to be with him! Proper attire and hair length required. Show up at 0800 hours, and don't be late! Directions to the church: From Main Street take a left, a left, a left, a right, and then a left."

CHILD: Daddy, that sounds scary!

DAD: You're probably right. Well, there's only one more: *[reading]* "Swing by Drive Thru Church of the Valley, where our motto is: 'Get in, get out, get on to lunch!' Receive your spiritual fill-up for the week and still beat the other denominations to the good restaurants! Communion is in individual to-go cups for people who need a sacrament on the run. You'll find our staff friendly and efficient, ready to meet your needs in 10 minutes or less. You can order your sermon CD in advance and have it ready to pick up so you can head out and to listen to the good news in your car. Value-size your order with bonus tracks including additional hymns and announcements."

CHILD: Whatever gets us to lunch faster. I'm hungry.

TEEN: Fast sounds good to me.

DAD: *[really beginning to lose optimism]* That just doesn't sound like a place where we can worship as a family.

MOM: *[looking at the ad]* It *is* right down the street, dear.

DAD: *[finally snaps]* Are you all serious? This is NOT what I had in mind!

MOM: But . . . where else are we going to go?

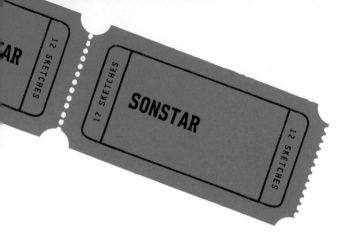

>>> PURPOSE:

Use this parody of an OnStar commercial to illustrate a discussion
about the peace and companionship Jesus brings people in a
lonely and uncertain world.

>>> POSSIBLE SCRIPTURES:

Psalm 23
Micah 5:4, 5
John 14
John 16:33

>>> PROPS:

five chairs
desk
desk phone or phone with headset
microphone

>>> PEOPLE:

Narrator—male or female; voice only
Operator—female; speaks kindly and calmly
Caller—male; obviously troubled

On one side of the stage, set up four chairs to represent a car. CALLER is sitting in driver's seat of the car. On the opposite side of the stage, set up a desk and another chair behind it, with the desk phone on the desk. OPERATOR is sitting behind the desk. NARRATOR is an offstage voice only, speaking through a microphone.

NARRATOR: The following is an actual call from a customer using the SonStar navigational system.

[CALLER is sitting in his car, frustrated. Before he says first line, CALLER looks around as if he can't find something. Then he pretends to punch something or does some other action to indicate frustration.]

CALLER: Are you kidding me? This *cannot* be happening! What am I gonna do? Who can even help me? Wait a minute . . . I've got SonStar now. I should try it out.

[CALLER pretends to press a button on his dashboard to activate his SonStar.]

OPERATOR: Hello. This is your SonStar operator. What is the nature of your emergency?

CALLER: They stole it! It's gone!

OPERATOR: Stolen? What has been stolen, sir?

CALLER: My whole life—my *life* has been stolen!

OPERATOR: Try to stay calm, sir. We *are* able to track your life with the SonStar system.

CALLER: I just want my life back.

OPERATOR: Of course.

CALLER: How does this work?

OPERATOR: Our navigation system can help you track your missing life, sir. First please tell me when you discovered your life was missing.

CALLER: Just now! I was going about my normal routine. Then all of a sudden I realized, I don't have a life anymore! I don't know when it even happened.

OPERATOR: We have some readings of recent locations of your life. Please stay on the line while I call them up on my screen.

CALLER: Thanks.

OPERATOR: Here we go. We show that a lot of your life has been found recently at 123 Main Street, in a residential house belonging to a Smith family. Does that sound familiar, sir?

CALLER: Uh, sure. That's Jack's house. I stop by there once in a while after school to blow off steam. Jack throws the best parties and always has a few . . . um, let's say *diversions* available to help people forget about their problems.

OPERATOR: We show your life there five times last week, sir.

CALLER: Yeah, it was a crazy week. Sometimes I just need to unwind, get away from my house, have some peace now and then. You know?

OPERATOR: Many people do lose their lives caught up in parties and substances, sir. But could I remind you that as a SonStar subscriber you have the Living Son to fill you with his Spirit? His Spirit is far superior to anything you'll find at the Smith residence, sir.

CALLER: Oh yeah?

OPERATOR: Yes, sir. I also see on my screen another address where your life has recently been found.

CALLER: Where?

OPERATOR: This appears to be a cyberspace location . . . www.R-U-Lonely.com?

CALLER: Uh . . . well, I guess I was there before.

OPERATOR: Our SonStar computer shows you there an average of four hours a day for the past two months.

CALLER: Sure. I guess so. I just need someone in my life. You know? Someone who'll be there for me.

OPERATOR: Again, sir, many people report losing their lives online. May I suggest that you use your privilege of being a SonStar subscriber to have the Living Son as a companion 24 hours a day, 7 days a week?

CALLER: That *would* be nice . . .

OPERATOR: And we also have found your life at a shopping complex on Twelfth and Elm.

CALLER: That would be the mall where I work. I got a second job recently.

OPERATOR: It is not uncommon for customers to lose their lives at work, sir.

CALLER: I know life isn't all about money, but I always seem to need some extra cash. I want to look good and have a little fun in life. I need money to do that.

OPERATOR: As a SonStar subscriber you *do* have the owner's "All These Things Added Unto You" guarantee, sir.

CALLER: What's that?

OPERATOR: The Living Son guarantees that all those things you *truly* need will be provided by him.

CALLER: That's great!

OPERATOR: Yes, sir. I believe we *can* recover your life for you. We suggest that you review your SonStar owner's agreement and read up on all the benefits of being a subscriber.

CALLER: I . . . I'll do that.

OPERATOR: Please do. We are glad to be of service.

NARRATOR: *[speaking a little quickly but distinctly to give this commercial wrap-up]* SonStar is a registered trademark of Resurrected Son Enterprises. All services are available for owners of any model of life in any country in the world. All costs have been paid by the owner more than 2,000 years ago. Read the section of the owner's agreement labeled "New Testament" for complete details.

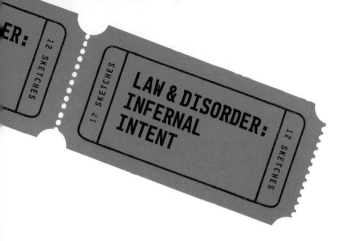

LAW & DISORDER: INFERNAL INTENT

12 SKETCHES

>>> PURPOSE:

Use this parody of *Law & Order: Criminal Intent* to illustrate a
discussion about the way demons may work in the world today.

>>> POSSIBLE SCRIPTURES:

Mark 9:14-29
Acts 19:13-16
1 Timothy 4:1-5
James 2:19

>>> PROPS:

business clothes for GORY and SCREAMS
good-luck charm such as a rabbit's foot or four-leaf clover
DVD case
2 books
bottle to represent beer

>>> PEOPLE:

ANNOUNCER
BOBBY GORY—a male demon; creepy and devious
AL-HEXANDRA SCREAMS—a female demon; creepy and devious

SUPERSTITIOUS GUY—nonspeaking role
CONFUSED GIRL—nonspeaking role
EATING DISORDER GIRL—nonspeaking role
ALCOHOLIC GUY—nonspeaking role

SUPERSTITIOUS GUY, CONFUSED GIRL, EATING DISORDER GIRL, and ALCOHOLIC GUY are spaced out across the stage, but EATING DISORDER GIRL and ALCOHOLIC GUY are near each other. All are frozen in position and unfreeze to pantomime their actions as the two demons stop beside them and talk about them. SUPERSTITIOUS GUY holds a good-luck charm or two and has a DVD at his feet. CONFUSED GIRL holds two books. ALCOHOLIC GUY has a beer bottle. BOBBY GORY and AL-HEXANDRA SCREAMS, dressed in business clothes, stand on one side of the stage, also frozen until their first line. ANNOUNCER is on opposite side of stage.

ANNOUNCER: On tonight's episode of *Law & Disorder: Infernal Intent,* watch criminal temptations being committed from the perspective of the tempters themselves—two demons named Bobby Gory and Al-Hexandra Screams. *[briefly pauses]* In Satan's ongoing war against humanity, a squad of elite tempters targets people in the 21st century. These are their stories. . . .

[GORY and SCREAMS unfreeze.]

GORY: Great to be back on temptation patrol together, Screams.

SCREAMS: Yeah, Gory. Just like when we were rookie demons.

GORY: So what cases are we on today?

[GORY and SCREAMS walk over to SUPERSTITIOUS GUY as he unfreezes and begins to look around as if paranoid. SUPERSTITIOUS GUY clings to his good-luck charms.]

SCREAMS: Our first is over here on Third Street—a high school sophomore we really have on the ropes.

GORY: How so?

SCREAMS: The kid is scared to death! While it's nice to have some people who don't believe we demons exist, this kid is just the opposite.

Gory: Let me guess. He thinks we're all-powerful, right?

Screams: Bingo! He has nightmares. He is becoming more and more superstitious. He won't step on a crack in the sidewalk. He runs from black cats. If the kid breaks a mirror, who knows what he'll do! The question is, how do we put on the pressure?

Gory: Well, I think Hollywood has helped us a lot here. How about a good slasher flick?

Screams: Will that help?

[Superstitious Guy picks up the DVD at his feet and begins to look at it.]

Gory: Think about. Kids die in those movies—usually kids who are guilty of something. And they die brutally. At the end of one movie, the maniac seems to be killed, but he keeps coming back. People die, but evil is eternal! The message of these movies is that evil overcomes everything! *[chuckles]*

Screams: But we know that's not true. We don't have a chance against anybody who trusts in the one who *really* came back from the dead.

Gory: And we'll keep that information away from this kid as long as possible, won't we?

Screams: You bet!

[Superstitious Guy freezes again. Gory and Screams walk over to Confused Girl as she unfreezes. Confused Girl looks at the two different books in her hands and appears distressed, trying to figure out which to believe.]

Gory: What else?

Screams: Well, we've got a real religious one over on Park Place.

Gory: Ouch!

Screams: Not to worry. I didn't tell you *what* religion!

Gory: Oh! You had me worried there.

Screams: The poor girl is so confused about silly arguments over pyramids and karma and prophecies . . . she is ready to give it all up!

GORY: Nice! She's doing all the work for us!

[CONFUSED GIRL freezes again. GORY and SCREAMS walk over to EATING DISORDER GIRL and ALCOHOLIC GUY as they unfreeze. EATING DISORDER GIRL pretends to throw up while ALCOHOLIC GUY pretends to drink beer.]

GORY: Well, that should fill up our morning. What do we have after lunch?

SCREAMS: We've got something really convenient—an apartment building on Washington. There's a couple thinking about divorce in 2C, a girl with an eating disorder in 4B, and alcoholics in 1F, 3D, and 5A!

GORY: Talk about one-stop shopping!

SCREAMS: Yep. Busy place.

GORY: So how are they dealing with their issues?

SCREAMS: The usual ways: flaky shrinks, the latest prescription meds, quizzes in women's magazines, and our old favorite . . .

GORY and SCREAMS: *[say in unison]* Good old self-reliance!

[EATING DISORDER GIRL and ALCOHOLIC GUY freeze again. GORY and SCREAMS walk a little farther and then stop.]

GORY: None of these people have any clue we're involved, do they?

SCREAMS: Not the foggiest. They blame their environments, their mothers, their genetic makeup. Demons are the last thing on their minds.

GORY: They figure if they just try harder or be around the right people or swallow the right chemical . . .

SCREAMS: *[finishes GORY's sentence]* Then *poof!*—all their problems will be gone!

GORY: Wow. How gullible can you get? They never see the spiritual causes of their problems.

SCREAMS: All in all, looks like an easy day.

GORY: Sure does.

SCREAMS: We probably didn't even need to start out this early.

GORY: True. How 'bout we stop for a donut?

SUMMER
VACATION

12 SKETCHES 12 SKETCHES 12 SKETCHES 12 SKETCHES

>>> **PURPOSE:**

Use this skit to illustrate a discussion about the causes of family conflict.

>>> **POSSIBLE SCRIPTURES:**

Genesis 25:19-34
Genesis 27
Genesis 37

>>> **PROPS:**

hair product of some sort to make ALLY's hair messed up
cell phone or cordless phone
bed or chairs set up to represent a bed; blanket and pillow
couch or chairs set up to represent a couch
remote control

>>> **PEOPLE:**

DAVE
ALLY
MOM

Stage is arranged as a bedroom on one side and living room on the other; remote control is on the couch. Scene opens with ALLY *asleep in bed.* DAVE *approaches her, phone in hand.*

DAVE: *[fake cheerful]* Oh Ally! Wake up, sis! It's summer vacation!

ALLY: *[wakes up groggily and has hilariously messy hair]* There's no school, so why am I waking up?

DAVE: *[dialing a phone number on the phone as he talks]* Because Brett Sanders, star of the school basketball team, is on the phone. *[shoves the phone to* ALLY's *ear and runs out of the bedroom area to the living room area, grabbing the remote control as he sits on the couch and pretending to turn on the TV]*

ALLY: *[yelling]* Get back here, you creep! Oh no, hi . . . um, not you, Mrs. Sanders. I was talking to my brother. I accidentally dialed the wrong number. Sorry to bother you. *[hangs up the phone and lays it on the bed, then heads to the living room area]* That's it! I've had it with you, Dave. *[yells offstage to* MOM*]* Mom! I can't share the same space with this annoyance any longer! Can't we trade him in for one of those St. Bernard dogs with the little barrel under its chin?

DAVE: Are you kidding? Mom would never allow a dirty, slobbering, unsanitary animal in this sterile house.

ALLY: She keeps *you,* doesn't she?

DAVE: I honestly don't know why you're so upset, Ally. It was just a joke.

ALLY: What if I run into Brett at the mall or something? He and his friends will laugh at me!

DAVE: And you aren't used to that by now? Just be glad he couldn't see you. *[laughing]* That's some nice bedhead you've got going on there. Is it spelling something?

ALLY: *[rubs her hands through her hair]* You're just asking because it spells a word longer than two letters, and you can't read it.

DAVE: Oooooo, this coming from a person who thought Julius Caesar was a salad dressing.

MOM: *[yells from offstage]* Would you two try to get along?

ALLY: *[yells offstage to* MOM*]* Aren't there any other options? *[to* DAVE*]* Dave, don't you have something better to do than watch TV?

DAVE: Like hole myself up in the bathroom with makeup and hair goo, staring at myself in the mirror for hours? Oops, that would be you, not me.

ALLY: At least I bathe! You hold the world's record for longest no-shower streak.

DAVE: *[self-righteously]* I don't waste water. *I'm* environmentally conscious.

ALLY: More like a walking biohazard.

DAVE: *[under his breath]* Hug a tree, plant your sister.

ALLY: What'd you say?

MOM: *[yells from offstage]* Hey! Are you two OK?

DAVE: *[yells offstage to MOM]* We're fine!

ALLY: *[sits down on the couch and puts her hand out]* Just give me the remote.

DAVE: *[hands ALLY the remote]* Fine, but I'm not watching those little prancing gymnasts.

ALLY: It's the Olympics!

DAVE: You can watch that anytime. Turn it to *The Price Is Right*. It's not the same since Bob Barker left, but it's still pretty good.

ALLY: The Summer Olympics only come around every four years!

DAVE: Kind of like your dates.

ALLY: Kind of like your brain.

DAVE: Kind of like your sense of humor. Turn to the Game Show Network. There are some classics on there. You should see how people used to dress in the '70s.

ALLY: You know, watching game shows is likely to change a person. Before long, you'll start knitting sweaters and eating nothing but TV dinners for weeks at a time.

DAVE: Like Aunt Marge?

ALLY: We don't even *have* an Aunt Marge! Who *are* you? We *aren't* watching any more of your dumb game shows.

DAVE: Is that your final answer?

[DAVE grabs for the remote, and the two begin wrestling for it. They should say things like "Gimme that!" "It's mine!" "We're watching MY show!" "No, we're watching MY show!" During this MOM enters, but DAVE and ALLY don't see her.]

MOM: *[puts hands on hips]* What are you two doing in here?

[DAVE and ALLY suddenly stop fighting and sit straight on the couch, answering immediately.]

DAVE AND ALLY: *[in unison]* Nothing!

MOM: *[sighs]* This is going to be a long summer.

>>> **PURPOSE:**

Use this parody of *Judge Judy* to illustrate a discussion about how Jesus fulfills God's law on our behalf.

>>> **POSSIBLE SCRIPTURES:**

Matthew 5:17-20
Romans 3
Hebrews 10:1-18

>>> **PROPS:**

robe for JUDGE TRULY (could use graduation robe or something similar)
table to represent judge's bench
chair
two smaller tables where plaintiff's LAWYER and defendant CHAD stand
three folders with papers inside
(optional) judge's gavel

>>> **PEOPLE:**

ANNOUNCER—male or female

JUDGE TRULY—a parody of Judge Judy; tough, no-nonsense woman with a New York accent

LAWYER—male or female

CHAD—typical high school teen who is in a band

A table with a chair behind it needs to be set up as the judge's bench. It should be the main focus on the stage, angled enough so that CHAD and LAWYER can stand before JUDGE TRULY without having their backs to the audience. If you have a gavel, it should be on JUDGE TRULY's bench. ANNOUNCER stands off to the side. As ANNOUNCER begins first line, JUDGE TRULY (wearing a robe) enters with a folder of paper and goes to her seat.

ANNOUNCER: *[to audience]* You are about the enter the courtroom of Judge Truly. The cases are real. The people are real. The judgment is FINAL!

[As ANNOUNCER says next line, CHAD and LAWYER enter, each carrying a folder with paper, and take their places behind the plaintiff and defendant tables.]

ANNOUNCER: *[to audience]* Today on *Judge Truly* . . . a large music company, Megabucks Music, is suing a teen musician for unpaid license fees.

[ANNOUNCER exits.]

JUDGE TRULY: *[looking in folder at papers]* Let's see what we have here. Megabucks Music v. Chad Simmons. *[to LAWYER]* Are you the attorney for Megabucks?

LAWYER: I am.

JUDGE TRULY: Go ahead and present your argument.

LAWYER: On July 16 of last year, the defendant and his associates were hired to perform music at a social gathering in a public park. At that time the defendant led his band, known as the . . . uh . . . *[looks in folder at papers]* Tree Squirrels, in performing a song to which Megabucks Music holds full title. Therefore, Megabucks is asking Mr. Simmons to pay the license fee for that song.

JUDGE TRULY: I see. And exactly what was this "social gathering"?

LAWYER: Your Honor, Mr. Simmons and his . . . Squirrels . . . were hired to play at a birthday party for a neighborhood 9-year-old.

JUDGE TRULY: And the song in question?

Lawyer: "Happy Birthday," Your Honor.

Judge Truly: I see on this complaint you are demanding that the defendant pay you $10,000 for playing your song.

Lawyer: That is our standard charge for a single public performance, Your Honor.

Judge Truly: Let me get this straight. You expect me to order a group of teenagers to pay you $10,000?

Lawyer: *[strongly]* We *expect* you to enforce the law!

Judge Truly: *[starting to fume]* You expect *me*? . . . Let me tell you, Counselor, I guarantee you don't push *me* around!

Lawyer: *[forcefully]* The law is the law, and this young man used our song without permission!

Judge Truly: *[retorting]* Don't hand me an ice cube and claim it sank the *Titanic*! We are talking about an amateur band playing at a children's party here!

Lawyer: *[more calmly]* Yes, Your Honor.

Judge Truly: Now let's hear from the defendant. Mr. Simmons?

Chad: Yes, Your Honor.

Judge Truly: Mr. Simmons, do you and your . . . Tree Squirrels . . . get hired to play often?

Chad: The birthday party was our first job, Your Honor.

Judge Truly: And you were paid for your services?

Chad: Yes, Your Honor. The band was paid $25.

Judge Truly: And I suppose all the cake you could eat?

Chad: No cake, Your Honor. Just $25.

Judge Truly: Tell me, Mr. Simmons, do you buy sheet music for the songs you perform?

Chad: No. We learn every song we play by ear, Your Honor.

Judge Truly: So you buy recordings of the artist's music so you can listen to them and learn them?

CHAD: Actually, Your Honor, we download the music from a site off the Internet. If we can't find what we want there, we borrow CDs from the local library and burn our own CDs.

JUDGE TRULY: So you don't pay *anything* for *any* of the music you play?

CHAD: That's right, Your Honor.

JUDGE TRULY: *[raised voice]* No, that is *not* right, young man! The artists who created the music deserve to get paid. You got paid, didn't you?

CHAD: Yes, Your Honor . . . $25 . . . *[trying to be funny]* No cake.

JUDGE TRULY: Mr. Simmons, your smart mouth may make you feel better, but it just makes *me* more irritated.

CHAD: Sorry.

JUDGE TRULY: You use someone else's music to earn money. Ripping CDs and illegal downloading are stealing. You are aware of that?

CHAD: But I don't think it's such a big deal to . . .

JUDGE TRULY: You *think*?! In this courtroom *my* opinion is the one that counts! Music piracy is serious business, whether you think so or not. Your freedom does not allow you to steal from someone else.

CHAD: *[pleading]* But everybody . . .

JUDGE TRULY: *[strongly]* Don't drive a getaway car and claim you're in a parade!

CHAD: *[quietly]* Huh?

JUDGE TRULY: Whether others commit the same crime is irrelevant, young man. We don't throw out the law because it isn't popular.

CHAD: Yes, Your Honor.

JUDGE TRULY: A law was broken, whether the Tree Squirrels recognized it or not. A fair price for the use of the music must be paid.

LAWYER: Thank you, Your Honor.

JUDGE TRULY: But of course, a teen band does not have the resources to pay the license fees Megabucks requires.

CHAD: No we don't, Your Honor.

JUDGE TRULY: Therefore, I am making this offer to you and your Squirrels, Mr. Simmons. I have recently invested in my own record label and need another band to record for me. My corporation will legally purchase all necessary licenses for the music you will perform. Also, if you agree to be my employees, the settlement with Megabucks will be worked out between them and my company.

[Both CHAD and LAWYER look surprised but happy. ANNOUNCER enters as JUDGE TRULY says her next line.]

JUDGE TRULY: *[If she has a gavel, she slams it now.]* Case dismissed, pending the acceptance of the terms by both parties.

[ANNOUNCER enters.]

ANNOUNCER: *[to audience]* Tomorrow on *Judge Truly* . . . an employee is accused of stealing from the coffee shop she works for.

JUDGE TRULY: *[to audience]* Don't fill my cup with dirty water and call it espresso!

ANNOUNCER: *[to audience]* See you in court!

>>> PURPOSE:

Use this parody of *Family Feud* to illustrate a discussion about the
blessings and assurance people have as children of God.

>>> POSSIBLE SCRIPTURES:

Galatians 3:23–4:7

>>> PROPS:

two long tables
a buzzer or similar item to make a negative sound effect to indicate a
wrong answer during the game show
a bell or similar item to make a positive sound effect to indicate a
correct answer during the game show

>>> PEOPLE:

Host
Carl Nell (pronounced similar to carnal)
Nell Family—three to four people, males and females
Chris Tonne (pronounced similar to Christian)
Tonne Family—three to four people, males and females
Prop Person—someone offstage to sound the buzzer and bell

Set up two tables on either side of the stage, angled slightly toward the center (emulating the stage on Family Feud*). Both families stand in a row behind the tables with* Carl *and* Chris *standing at the ends of their tables the farthest from the audience.* Host *stands in the center between the two families. All lines written for* Nell Family *and* Tonne Family *are improvised, and the family members usually all talk at once; suggestions are given for typical lines to say.*

Host: Hello, everyone, and welcome back to *Kinfolk Clash*. We have Carl Nell and his relatives versus Chris Tonne and his clan. The next question on our show goes to the Carl Nell family. *[steps over to* Carl*]* Are you and your kinfolk ready, Mr. Nell?

Carl: Let's go!

Nell Family: *[to* Carl *and each other]* Yeah, let's go! We can do it! We've got this! Etc.

Host: All right. You know the rules: your answers must match our top five survey answers on the board or you'll get a strike. Three strikes and all the points go to your opponents, the Chris Tonne family. Now, 100 heavenly angels were asked this question: *How do people earn salvation from God?*

Nell Family: *[to* Carl*]* Go to church. Read the Bible. Don't smoke. Keep the Ten Commandments. Care for the needy. Etc.

Host: I need an answer, Carl.

Carl: OK. How about "Keeping the Ten Commandments"?

Nell Family: *[to* Carl *and each other]* Yeah! Good answer! Etc.

Host: OK. Let's see if "Keeping the Ten Commandments" is up there. Survey says . . .

*[*Prop Person *sounds the buzzer.* Carl *and* Nell Family *groan, sigh, and look disappointed.]*

Host: Sorry. That's one strike. Do you want to make another guess, or do you want to pass to your opponents?

Nell Family: *[to* Carl *and each other]* Play! We'll play. Let's go for it. Etc.

Carl: We'll play.

Host: All right. Five answers remain on the board. I need you to give me one.

Carl: *[to Family]* What do you guys think?

Nell Family: Go to church. Yeah, that's a good one. Try it. Etc.

Carl: *[to Host]* OK. We'll say "Go to church."

Nell Family: *[to Carl and each other]* Yeah! Good answer! Etc.

Host: OK. Let's see if "Go to church" is up there. Survey says:

[Prop Person sounds the buzzer. Carl and Nell Family groan, sigh, and look disappointed.]

Host: That's two strikes. Do you want to try another guess or see if Chris and his family are also stumped?

Nell Family: Pass! They'll never get it. Let them try! Etc.

Carl: We'll pass.

Host: *[walks over to Chris]* All right. Let's go to the Chris Tonnes. Mr. Tonne, do you have an answer?

[Tonne Family nods.]

Chris: I think we're all sure of this one. We'll say "Accept God's grace through Jesus."

Tonne Family: *[to Chris and each other]* Yeah! Good answer! Etc.

Host: OK. Let's look for it!

[Prop Person sounds the bell five times. Chris and Tonne Family cheer.]

Host: Well, it looks like you got *all* the top five answers with that *one* response! *[walks over to Nell Family]* Back to the Nell family. Let's see if you guys can give one of these top three answers. Again, 100 heavenly angels were asked this question: *What kind of people do you expect to find in Heaven?*

Nell Family: Good people. Americans. Good citizens. Little old ladies. Rich people. Generous people. Etc.

Host: I need an answer, Carl.

CARL: OK. How about "Good people"?

NELL FAMILY: *[to CARL and each other]* Yeah! Good answer! Etc.

HOST: OK. Let's see if "Good people" is up there." Survey says:

[PROP PERSON sounds the buzzer. CARL and NELL FAMILY groan, sigh, and look disappointed.]

HOST: Sorry. That's one strike. Do you want to make another guess, or do you want to pass to your opponents?

[CARL and NELL FAMILY look frustrated.]

CARL: *[disgusted]* Just let 'em have it.

HOST: All right. *[walks over to CHRIS]* Back to the Chris Tonnes. Mr. Tonne, do you have an answer?

CHRIS: How about "People from every race"?

TONNE FAMILY: *[to CHRIS and each other]* Yeah! Good answer! Etc.

HOST: OK. Let's see how you did! Show me "People from every race."

[PROP PERSON sounds the bell once. CHRIS and TONNE FAMILY cheer.]

HOST: Do you have another answer?

CHRIS: How about "Both males and females"?

TONNE FAMILY: *[to CHRIS and each other]* Yeah! Good answer! Etc.

HOST: Let's see it. Survey says:

[PROP PERSON sounds the bell once. CHRIS and TONNE FAMILY cheer.]

HOST: "Men and women" is up there! That's good. One answer remains. Do you have a guess?

CHRIS: How about "All walks of life, like rich *and* poor people"?

TONNE FAMILY: *[to CHRIS and each other]* Yeah! Good answer! Etc.

[PROP PERSON sounds the bell once. CHRIS and TONNE FAMILY cheer.]

HOST: You swept the board. Congratulations! Now back to the Carl Nells one more time. Carl, one category remains. Are you up for this?

CARL: *[dejected]* We'll try.

HOST: Carl Nell and his family will have one more chance to put points on the board here on *Kinfolk Clash* . . . right after this brief word from our sponsors.

NOT HERE
RIGHT NOW

12 SKETCHES

>>> **PURPOSE:**

Use this skit to illustrate a discussion about the difference it would make if people allowed Jesus to direct their lives.

>>> **POSSIBLE SCRIPTURES:**

Psalm 121
Isaiah 9:6
Isaiah 11:1-5

>>> **PROPS:**

four cell phones

>>> **PEOPLE:**

STEPHANIE—popular girl
SCOTT WILLIAM SANDERS—preppy and political guy
MISTRESS MYRNA—psychic, speaks with a Jamaican accent
DESMOND Q. NERDLY—inventor, speaks in a computer-sounding voice

The characters should be spread out on the stage. You may choose to have them standing with their backs to the audience until it is their turn to speak. Or you may choose to have them freeze in position until it is their turn.

The characters should have cell phones up to their ears as they speak. Their lines are supposed to be voice-mail messages. At the end of each message, the character should say "BEEP," pretending to be the signal for someone to leave a message.

STEPHANIE: Hi, this is Stephanie—prom queen of Hoovertown High! I'm not able to grab my phone right now. I may be getting my hair done. Or I may be out on a date. Or I may be screening my calls, deciding if I want to talk to you! But leave your name and a message and I'll try to find time to call you back. And guys—please leave your first *and* last names. After all, I need to know *which* Mike, Matt, or Benjamin to call back! *BEEP!*

SCOTT: *[hums a few bars of patriotic/march music]* Welcome to the Scott William Sanders campaign headquarters. Scott William Sanders is not available to talk right now, but he *does* want to be your next student council president. Have a complaint about school lunches? Have an idea for the destination of your senior trip? Why not tell Scott William Sanders?! Strong political leadership will get things done, and you can trust Scott William Sanders for that leadership. So leave your message in the capable hands of Scott William Sanders. I am Scott William Sanders, and I approve this message. *BEEP!*

MYRNA: *[in a Jamaican accent]* You have reached da offices of Mistress Myrna, queen of da psychics. Ta have an astrological chart prepared, press 1 now. Ta schedule a séance, rap twice and levitate 2 inches off da floor. Ta request holistic healing, drink three cups of wormwood tea and call me in the morning. Ta complain about a psychic reading dat did not turn out da way you would like, do *not* leave ya name and number. I *know* who ya are, and I *know* where ya live. *BEEP!*

DESMOND: *[monotone, computer-sounding voice]* Your call is being handled by the fully automated answering and response system of Desmond Q. Nerdly. The electronic signature of your telephone transmission is being analyzed at this moment by Nerdly Communi-bot 5.3. It will match your identity to one of the entries in its database. A suitable response will be formulated and automatically sent to your e-mail address by the time you hang up from this call. We are proud to announce that this system is able to respond to all calls within 7.8 seconds with an amazing 99.89 percent rate of accuracy . . . *[makes static sound as if disconnected]*

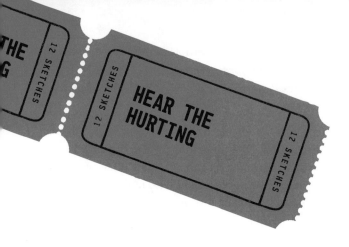

HEAR THE HURTING

>>> PURPOSE:

Use this readers' theater script to illustrate a discussion about what people can do to can help others who are hurting.

>>> POSSIBLE SCRIPTURES:

Job 2:11-13
Matthew 25:34-40
Romans 12:15

>>> PROPS:

>>> PEOPLE:

READER 1
READER 2
READER 3
READER 4

Readers' Theater is a type of drama that allows the actors to hold their scripts and read the lines dramatically. There are no costumes or props, only people standing on the stage, facing the audience, reading the lines and trying to convey the emotion of the words. The actors should read the lines one right after the other, sometimes in unison where indicated. There can be a slight pause after each unison line.

READER 1: I was hurt.

READER 2: I was angry.

READER 3: I was devastated.

READER 4: I was miserable.

ALL: And I was all alone.

READER 1: There was no one.

READER 2: No one who cared.

READER 3: No one who would listen.

READER 4: No one who understood.

ALL: Just me.

READER 1: I never thought it would happen to me. My heart was ripped in two.

READER 2: I was betrayed by someone I trusted. Who could I turn to?

READER 1: Can't you see how bad it makes me feel?

READER 2: Can you blame me for being mad?

READER 3: All my dreams were crushed into little pieces.

READER 4: I messed up. I know. But that doesn't make it any easier.

READER 3: What's the point anymore?

READER 4: What am I supposed to do now?

ALL: How can I go on?

READER 1: Don't act like you know how I feel. You don't know how it hurts.

READER 2: Don't try to be my friend *now*. It's too late.

READER 1 AND READER 2: Leave me alone!

READER 3: Don't say it's OK . . . because it's not!

READER 4: Don't look at me that way. It happened. Just forget it.

READER 3 AND READER 4: Go away!

READER 1: Where is God anyway?

READER 2: Isn't he supposed to be here for me?

READER 3: Why didn't he stop it from happening?

READER 4: Why won't he answer me?

ALL: Maybe God just doesn't care.

>>> **PURPOSE:**

Use this parody of a dating game show to illustrate a discussion about
Wicca and its elevation of nature and how those beliefs differ
from Christianity.

>>> **POSSIBLE SCRIPTURES:**

Genesis 1:26, 27
Genesis 3:17, 18
Psalm 8:4-8
Psalm 90:2, 3
Romans 8:20-22

>>> **PROPS:**

three stools or chairs
(optional) wall or screen, some type of barrier to divide the stage

>>> **PEOPLE:**

HOST—male or female
JASMINE—show contestant
WILL—follower of Wicca
BRADLEY—follower of Jesus

JASMINE should be seated on a stool toward the front left side of the stage. HOST should stand beside her. WILL and BRADLEY should be seated on stools on the right side of the stage, a little farther back from the front so that JASMINE cannot see them as she is sitting. If you have a barrier, put it up in the middle of the stage so JASMINE definitely cannot see WILL and BRADLEY.

HOST: Good evening from all of us here on the show *Truth or Counterfeit!* The goal of our game is for one contestant to determine which facts represent the truth about God and the natural world and which facts are spiritual counterfeits. All the contestant has to do is ask the right questions. Today's player is a student from Yourtown, Mississippi. Welcome, Jasmine!

JASMINE: *[waves and smiles to audience]* Hi.

HOST: Jasmine, you know how our game works. Sitting just out of your sight are representatives of two very different religious groups. You will ask three questions and *only* three questions to each guest. On the basis of those answers, you'll see if you can separate the truth from the counterfeit. Are you ready, Jasmine?

JASMINE: As ready as I'll ever be, I guess!

HOST: That's great! But before you ask your first question, let me introduce our guests, Will and Bradley, to our audiences at home and in the studio. It's a secret to you, Jasmine, so cover your ears!

[JASMINE covers her ears as HOST walks over to stand by WILL and BRADLEY. HOST speaks in a stage whisper.]

HOST: *[points to WILL]* Guest number 1 is Will. Will is a member of a local coven of Wicca, modern-day witchcraft. He is our counterfeit guest. *[points to BRADLEY]* Guest number 2 is Bradley, a Bible-believing member of First Church, and he represents the truth.

[HOST walks back over to JASMINE and has her uncover her ears.]

HOST: Now that the audience knows which guy is which, it's your turn to figure them out. Let's have your first question, Jasmine!

JASMINE: OK. Here goes . . . This question is for Will. I find some religious people very judgmental. How will you make me feel good about myself?

WILL: Jasmine, I know just how you feel. You won't hear words like *sin* and *eternal salvation* from me! Those are really outdated terms. I won't try to scare you with talk of the devil or Hell. You need someone who allows you to be yourself and doesn't force his morality on you. I'll let you do whatever your inner spirit tells you to do, as long as you do not hurt someone else.

JASMINE: Wow! I kind of like that! Bradley, same question . . .

BRADLEY: Jasmine, there is a difference between being judgmental and being honest. You need someone who loves you enough to tell you the truth. The truth is that because you are a human being, you are a glorious creature! You share the very nature of the one who created you. But . . . we all do things that hurt each other, even when we think we won't. You need a standard of right and wrong that applies to everyone and doesn't vary with your feelings from day to day. And you need someone who loves you enough to help you with those standards you find difficult to keep.

JASMINE: Hmmm . . . interesting. Let's go on. I'll stick with Bradley for a moment. Bradley, you tell me God is a friend of yours. So how will you introduce him to me?

BRADLEY: Good question, Jasmine. I want you to think about something. Since we agree that God is so much greater and more complex than us, meeting him could be difficult, couldn't it? God talking to us would be like a human being talking to an animal. But what if a human being could *become* an animal? Then the message could be communicated much more easily. That's what God did. He became a human being called Jesus. I would introduce you to God by introducing you to what is written about Jesus in the Bible.

JASMINE: I see. Will, what do you think about Jesus?

WILL: I think learning about God by learning about Jesus is fine. Or you could learn about Zeus or Odin. And why be sexist about it? Why not learn about Aphrodite and Artemis and Athena? Women should certainly get equal time! Jasmine, the fact is, God is too big for any of us to really know. "The All" is the spirit that flows from all living things. It is good to put a human face on God. But don't think of "The All" as a person. It's like surfing. You don't introduce yourself to the waves—you get into the flow of the waves and let them carry you along. I will help you attune yourself to the natural rhythm of life.

JASMINE: I see . . . So Will, I take it that you are an outdoorsy sort of guy. I'm concerned about the environment. Are you?

WILL: You bet! We can't be arrogant humans who think we own this planet. We share the earth with the spirits of every living plant and animal. We need to embrace nature and learn from our beautiful world.

JASMINE: Bradley, what do you think about nature?

BRADLEY: Jasmine, we live in a beautiful world. But we also live in a dangerous world. I love the beach on a sunny day, but I wouldn't be there during a hurricane! Lions and tigers are majestic creatures, but I know enough to keep my distance or I'll truly become "one with nature"! Nature is beautiful. But it is not perfect. It was once, and a new world is coming that will be again. We need to respect nature but not treat it as if it were divine.

HOST: As you know, Jasmine, that was your last question. Are you ready to make your decision?

JASMINE: Wow. This is hard. They both sounded so sincere.

HOST: I'm sure they did. But the moment of truth is almost here. Ladies and gentlemen, join us as Jasmine tries to tell truth from counterfeit, right after these words from our sponsors.

>>> PURPOSE:

Use this parody of VH1's *Behind the Music* to illustrate a discussion about how biblical principles can help people make good decisions.

>>> POSSIBLE SCRIPTURES:

Psalm 37:4
Proverbs 15:22
1 Corinthians 10:23-32
Colossians 3:17

>>> PROPS:

ball cap, shirt, and jeans for JayJay
microphone
trendy jacket
sunglasses
fake beer
fake cigar
gold necklace
fancy coat (think leather or fur)
Bible

NARRATOR—male or female
JAYJAY—male; nonspeaking role
MOM—female
MANAGER—male
COUSIN—male or female

The NARRATOR should be standing off to one side of the stage. At center stage on the floor, place the microphone, trendy jacket, sunglasses, fake beer, fake cigar, gold necklace, fancy coat, and Bible that JAYJAY will later need. JAYJAY will begin by wearing some sort of shirt, jeans, and a ball cap. Once he enters, he will stand center stage throughout. MOM enters as NARRATOR begins first lines and should stand on the opposite side of the stage from NARRATOR. When it is time for the other two characters to speak, they will enter and stand beside MOM. All characters remain onstage once they enter.

NARRATOR: You've heard his music climb to the top of the charts. Now discover JayJay Mac's rocky road to stardom in this edition of *Behind the Musician: Making of a Hip-Hop Star.* JayJay Mac was born Jerome Jordan Maxwell to a family who taught him to reach for his dreams but keep his feet on the ground.

[JAYJAY enters, dressed and acting as a little kid, hat sideways, jeans rolled up to be short. He goes to center stage. As MOM describes what JAYJAY did as a kid, JAYJAY should do those things: pretending to sing in front of the mirror and practicing his dance moves.]

MOM: I always knew my baby would be a star. Ever since he was a kid, he'd be writing lyrics that he'd sing in the shower. Then he'd get in front of our living room mirror and strut his stuff, trying to practice his dance skills. He always said he would make it big. Now, I believed he had the talent, but I worried that success would go to the poor boy's head. And it did—way too fast.

[As NARRATOR speaks, MANAGER enters and stands beside MOM. JAYJAY rolls jeans back down, turns his cap backward, and picks up microphone.]

NARRATOR: When JayJay was 17, he won first prize at a local karaoke competition, which landed him a recording contract.

[As MANAGER speaks, JAYJAY pretends to sing dramatically.]

MANAGER: I remember the night I first discovered JayJay. He was like a thousand other kids, thinking they're bigger and better than they are. They get all this reality TV, *American Idol* stuff in their minds and think anybody can be a star overnight. They don't realize the hard work involved. JayJay was no different. But the kid had talent. I'm telling you, he was something special. I thought he might be worth investing in. He was, but it sure was more difficult than I thought to rein him in.

[As MOM speaks, JAYJAY lays down the microphone, takes off his cap and lays it down, and puts on the jacket and sunglasses. He crosses his arms over his chest as if he is a superstar.]

MOM: I was proud that Jerome had won that contest, but I reminded him to be realistic. One-hit wonders are a dime a dozen. I tell you, it broke this mother's heart when he dropped out of school. He just had one year left, and he blew it off to chase after his big dream.

[As NARRATOR speaks, COUSIN enters to stand beside MOM, while JAYJAY picks up the fake beer and cigar. JAYJAY pretends there are tons of people surrounding him, as if he is partying and the center of attention, drinking and smoking.]

NARRATOR: Like countless musicians before him, JayJay Mac scored it big with his first hit. He lived the superstar lifestyle for a while.

COUSIN: When cousin JayJay came home for Thanksgiving, he was a different person. Now that he had millions of fans, he barely had time for the people who truly cared about him. He acted like he was too good for us. We used to hang out all the time, but JayJay got new friends. He started partying with the wrong crowd, drinking, doing drugs, and chasing girls. I tried to confront him when he actually stopped by on Thanksgiving for a few minutes. I told him his mama didn't raise him that way. He knew better. I told him his family and the God he said he loved expected better out of him. JayJay pushed me away and told me I didn't understand and I didn't fit into his life anymore.

[As MANAGER speaks, JAYJAY lays down the fake beer and cigar, takes off jacket and lays it down, and puts on the gold necklace and fancy coat. JAYJAY picks up

the fake beer and cigar again, partying more and acting as if he's too good for anyone.]

MANAGER: JayJay's star burned bright for a while . . . and quickly went out. I've seen it time and time again in this industry. We worked hard to get him gigs, but JayJay got tossed aside when the next big star came along. JayJay couldn't handle the rejection, and he lost it. He partied harder and blew off all the events I set up for him. I'd about had it. I'd seen enough of these teen stars to know when it was time to cut out and go. I'd fulfilled my contract with JayJay, and I was about ready to leave. I'd done all I could do as his manager. So I gave him an ultimatum—clean up your act or go back to being a nobody.

[As NARRATOR speaks, JAYJAY takes off coat, necklace, and sunglasses and lays them down, and pulls his pockets out from his jeans to indicate he has lost all his money. JAYJAY sits down on the floor, head in hands, looking miserable.]

NARRATOR: Like many teen stars before him, JayJay's life spiraled down to rock bottom.

MOM: The tears I cried as I saw my little boy fall apart! I prayed and prayed for his soul every night, asking the Lord to get his attention. Desperate, I called Jerome one night and said he had ripped out my heart. I said he'd been given a gift by God Almighty and he was throwing it all down the drain. I hung up that night, vowing not to speak to him again until he decided to get his life back on track.

[As NARRATOR speaks, JAYJAY remains seated but puts pockets back into jeans and picks up the Bible and begins to read it.]

NARRATOR: The tough love and prayers by his family and manager brought JayJay Mac back from the depths. He put himself in a rehab facility and came out a new man. He got his GED and chose to use his musical talent for a higher calling.

[As COUSIN speaks, JAYJAY remains seated reading Bible and now begins to smile.]

COUSIN: It was so cool when JayJay walked through the door the next time. He was back to being the cousin I knew and loved! He was on fire for his family and for Jesus again. He told me that from now on, his lyrics and his life would be a testimony to God's greatness.

[As MANAGER speaks, JAYJAY stands up with the Bible in hand and pretends to sing to God, while holding arm up to Heaven.]

MANAGER: You'd think in this day and age that only trashy songs would sell albums. Record labels certainly think so. But JayJay proved that wrong. Listeners are hungry for something real, and that's what JayJay Mac is all about. His songs speak his reality—which reflects a love of Jesus and love for people. He really wants people to know that he cares and God cares. It's great to hear positive lyrics played on both Christian and secular radio stations. JayJay's not the kid I saw singing karaoke years ago. He's become a man now.

[As NARRATOR speaks, JAYJAY puts down the Bible and walks over to where MOM, MANAGER, and COUSIN are standing. They all smile, hug him, pat him on the back, etc., and pantomime talking together.]

NARRATOR: JayJay Mac, hip-hop artist with a mission, has chosen his path in life and is walking the road to true success. And that's all for this week's edition of *Behind the Musician*.

DIRECTOR'S CUT

Drama can be used in a variety of settings to spark imagination. Here is an example of how we'd use "Hometown Idol" (page 7) to illustrate a devotion about rejection. Open your session with the skit. Then make the following devotional presentation:

We've all seen how *American Idol* contestants react when they are rejected. That's part of the reason why people watch the show's first episodes, wondering how odd or angry people will respond when they are turned away. Although some people act a bit overdramatic for the TV cameras, it is true that being rejected in any form cause bitterness. Anger, frustration, and despair often result when a person feels rebuffed. How can we learn to handle rejection more like Samantha in our skit? Let's look at another "Sam"—Samuel, the last judge of Israel. God tells us in the Bible that Samuel also experienced rejection. But he overcame bitterness when he learned to extract, examine, and express.

EXTRACT 1 SAMUEL 8:1-5
SEPARATE YOUR PERSONAL FEELINGS FROM THE ISSUE AT HAND.

Israel was different from any other nation that ever existed. When the people marched through the wilderness, a king did not lead them, but rather the cloud of God's presence over the tabernacle (Exodus 40:36-38). It was not a king that gave the nation its laws, but God (Exodus 20:1). After Israel had settled into the promised land, no human king ruled, but God deputized judges to be his agents to lead and protect his nation (Judges 2:16). The only king of Israel was Jehovah God.

Samuel was one of these judges and was respected for his godliness. But Samuel's sons were another matter. Joel and Abijah used whatever power they had for themselves (1 Samuel 8:1-3). Near the end of Samuel's life, the elders of Israel went to Samuel, asking him to step down and judge and to "appoint a king to lead us, such as all the other nations have" (vv. 4, 5).

Imagine being asked to give up an office held successfully for years and years. Such rejection surely hurt Samuel. But he took steps to keep from letting rejection make him bitter. The first step was to analyze the situation as unemotionally as possible. When he did so, it was clear that the real issue was not his loss of a job. The real issue was that the elders among the people were willing to let uncertainty about the future convince them to be like the other nations, rather than be the nation God called them to be.

In our skit, Samantha did not dwell on Silas's hurtful words. She realized that his mean temper was his issue, not hers. Instead, she looked for constructive criticism in the situation and moved on.

EXAMINE 1 SAMUEL 8:6-8
SEEK GOD'S PERSPECTIVE ON THE ISSUE AT HAND.

Samuel took his feelings of rejection to God. God responded to Samuel's prayer, basically saying, "It's not about you" (1 Samuel 8:6, 7). God reminded Samuel that this was not unusual behavior for Israel. From the day God had brought the Israelites up out of Egypt they had been whining, disobeying, and turning to worship other gods (v. 8). Rejection is an emotional experience. Emotions, however, are ever changing, and are never a solid basis for taking action. God's Word, on the other hand, is an unchanging touchstone.

Other biblical characters discovered this fact when they went through rejection. Job's loss of family, health, and wealth left him frustrated and angry. He questioned God's justice and asked for a response—in writing (Job 31:35). God did one better and answered out of the storm (Job 38:1, 2). Jeremiah was upset when he saw faithless people having an easier life than he (Jeremiah 12:1). The prophet listened when God answered, telling him to toughen up (v. 6). Paul feared for his life in the hostile, pagan environment of Corinth, but God eased his fears, giving Paul the comfort to stay there for another year and a half (Acts 18:9-11).

When we are rejected, we need to allow God's Word to evaluate, and if necessary, correct our emotional response. The written Word of God and the counsel of other Christians can be very helpful during these times. Samantha remembered God's command to make a joyful noise from Psalm 100:1. This allowed her to recognize that the privilege to praise God eternally was far more important than temporary fame.

EXPRESS 1 SAMUEL 8:9, 10, 19-22
HAVE YOUR SAY AND MOVE ON.

God told Samuel to allow the people to select a king, but to also warn them of the consequences of that choice (2 Samuel 8:9). Samuel offered a powerful, well thought-out defense of God's will in this matter. "When that day comes," concluded Samuel, "you will cry out for relief . . . and the Lord will not answer you" (vv. 10-18).

Despite this clear presentation of truth, the elders held their ground. They insisted on having a king so they could be like all the other nations (vv. 19-20). Samuel's response should be a model for all of us. He didn't argue, but went to the Lord, and let it drop.

The fact is, just because we are right doesn't guarantee that people will do the right thing. When Jesus sent out his disciples to preach, he warned that some would not listen. But rather than argue, the disciples were to "shake the dust off [their] feet" and move on (Matthew 10:14). When the synagogue leaders in Corinth became abusive to Paul, "he shook out his clothes in protest" (Acts 18:6). When we are rejected, we need to learn not to whine. We just need to say what God wants us to say and move on. Notice that in our skit, Samantha did not pout or scream as some have in such shows sometimes. She calmly stated her position and moved on.

People who have suffered rejection have reacted with bitterness and even violence. But those who trust God can attempt to separate their emotions from the situation, seek God's counsel, find closure, and move on. Let's follow the example set by Samuel—and Samantha.

INDEX BY TOPIC

INDEX BY SCRIPTURE

Don't miss the other two books in the SKITS FOR STUDENT MINISTRY series!

12 SKETCHES — 12 SKETCHES

RETELL
BIBLE NARRATIVES
FROM ANOTHER ANGLE

Includes parodies of TV shows such as *The Real World, CSI,* and *So You Think You Can Dance* while looking into topics such as purity, leadership, suffering, God's mercy, and more!

INTRODUCE
BIBLE TOPICS
FROM ANOTHER ANGLE

Includes parodies of TV shows such as *The Amazing Race* and *SportsCenter* while looking into topics such as respect in dating, materialism, prayer, emotions, and more!

Contact your local Christian Supplier, call 1-800-543-1353 or visit www.standardpub.com